W9-AWY-840

Beans

by Gail Saunders-Smith

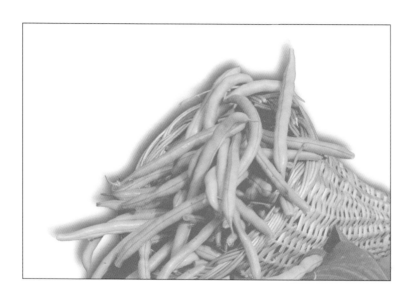

Pebble Books

an imprint of Capstone Press

Pebble Books

Pebble Books are published by Capstone Press
151 Good Counsel Drive, P.O. Box 669, Mankato, Minnesota 56002
http://www.capstone-press.com

2 3 4 5 6 7 07 06 05 04 03

Library of Congress Cataloging-in-Publication Data
Saunders-Smith, Gail.
   Beans / by Gail Saunders-Smith.
   p. cm.—(Plants)
   Summary: Photographs and simple text depict planting, growing, picking, and
eating green beans.
   ISBN 1-56065-487-2 (hardcover)
   ISBN 1-56065-946-7 (paperback)
   1. Beans—Juvenile literature. 2. Beans—Life cycles—Juvenile literature.
[1. Beans.] I. Title. II. Series.
   SB327.S28 1997
   635'.652—dc21   97-23585

Editorial Credits

Lois Wallentine, editor; Timothy Halldin and James Franklin,
designers; Michelle L. Norstad, photo researcher

Photo Credits

David F. Clobes, 4, 18
Winston Fraser, 10
Dwight Kuhn, cover, 3, 8
Unicorn Stock/Joel Dexter, 12; Eric Berndt, 14; Ted
   Rose, 1, 16; Karen Holsinger Mullen, 20

Table of Contents

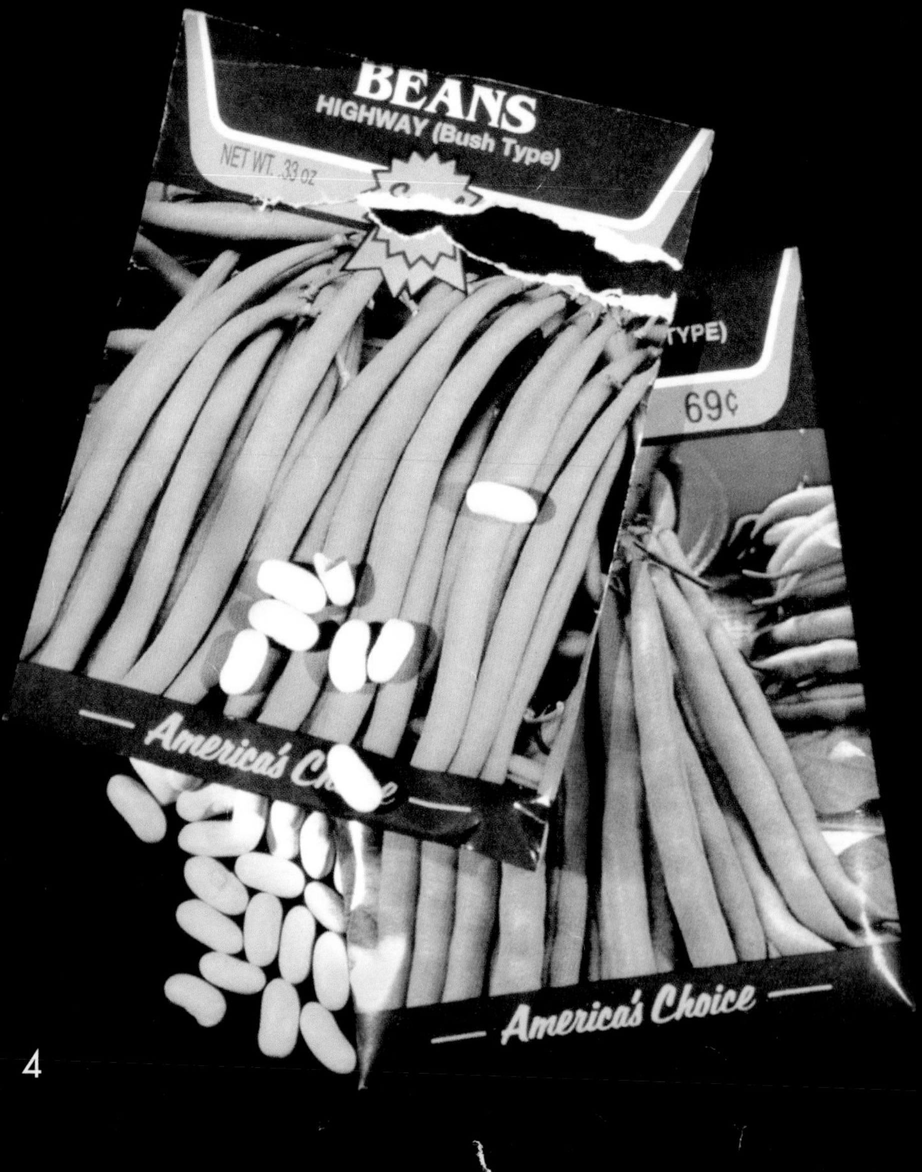

seeds in a packet

seeds in a pod

seeds in a hole

beans in a garden

bean blossom

bean pod

beans in a basket

beans in a bowl